The Art of Handmade Flowers

Step-By-Step Instructions for
Over 70 Beautiful Nylon Creations

Jue Liu

New Sheer Creations
www.NewSheer.com

ISBN-13 978-0-9824109-0-5
ISBN-10 0-9824109-0-5
Library of Congress Control Number: 2009937599

The Art of Handmade Flowers

Editor: Janice Wei

Translator: Dawn Wang

Text Editor: Clyde Wright

Copy Editor: Fe Canono, Samantha Clements

Cover Design: JAM Graphics Design, Oakland CA

Printed in China

For additional information, please contact:

New Sheer Creations
Pleasanton, California USA
Email: contact@newsheer.com
Website: www.newsheer.com

The *Art* of
HANDMADE FLOWERS

C o n t e n t s

Q Some Basics about Nylon Flowers A

Q What is nylon flower?

A The art of nylon flower-making (also known as "stocking" flowers) enjoyed a brief popularity in the United States in the '70s and soon became very popular in Japan. In recent years, the craft's popularity has spread to other parts of Asia and Australia. It is an easy to learn craft which uses simple tools and inexpensive materials to achieve stunning results. The introduction of new colors and materials has added infinite new possibilities to the art of nylon flower-making. This book utilizes the latest materials and techniques to create realistic and artful flowers and arrangements.

Q What materials are needed to make nylon flowers?

A The basic materials needed to make nylon flowers include: wire, stem wire, nylon stocking, nylon threading, floral tape and stamen. Some flowers require cotton balls or sheets (or you can use batting), white glue, acrylic paint and paint brushes.

Wire is used to construct the frame of the flower. The wire used for nylon flower is very pliable and comes in different thickness (gauge), 18, 20, 22, 24, 26, 28, 30, etc. The higher the gauge number, the thinner the wire. #20 and #22 gauge wires are made with a very thin layer of paper on the outside. These lower gauge wires come mostly in white, green and brown and are generally used for thin flower stem or leaf stem. #24, #26 and #28 gauge wires are coated with a thin layer of plastic or are spray painted. They come in a variety of colors, such as gold, silver, red, green, blue, and yellow. #24 and #26 gauge wires are most suitable for making the frames for flower petals and leaves.

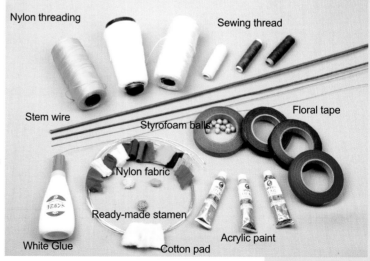

Nylon threading • Sewing thread • Stem wire • Styrofoam balls • Floral tape • Nylon fabric • White Glue • Ready-made stamen • Cotton pad • Acrylic paint

Stem wire is used to make the stem. Stem wires come in thin and thick. They are made from different thickness of wire, and then coated with white, green or brown paper.

Nylon Stocking is used to make flower petal or leaves. It is the same material used to make panty hose. The nylon material is tubular in shape and comes in single and dual-colors. Dual color stockings use a 2-colors blend, creating a tie-dye effect. Both single and dual-color stockings come in a wide range of shades.

Stamen and Pistil are the reproductive organs of a flower. Stamen is the component and pistil is the female contingent. Most flowers have stamens and pistils with very distinct colors, shapes, and number of filaments. Ready-made stamens/pistils are typically shaped like match sticks and come in a variety of sizes and colors. There are also a few specialized stamens available on the market, such as button-shaped. Stamens and pistils can be handmade to achieve the most realistic results for some flowers and are also fun to make.

Nylon Threading is a type of threading that is used to tie the nylon onto the wire frames, bind the petals together and attach them to the stems. The stretching characteristics of the nylon threading enable a tight tie that does not need to be knotted for a durable bond.

Floral Tape has a waxy feel and has a bit of elasticity. It is widely used in making flower-arrangements. In nylon flower making, it also works as a glue to hold petals together to create flowers and attach them to the stems. Floral tape is available in a variety of colors, such as red, white, yellow, brown, green, and light green.

Q What tools are needed to make nylon flowers?

A The basic tools used to make nylon flowers include wire cutters or diagonal cutting pliers, long-nose craft pliers or flat-nose craft pliers, and scissors. To make the loops for petals and leaves, common household items in cylindrical shapes can be utilized as guides, such as bottles of various sizes. There are also

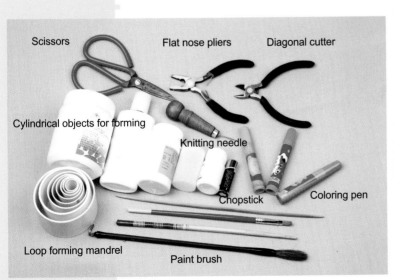

Scissors — Flat nose pliers — Diagonal cutter — Cylindrical objects for forming — Knitting needle — Chopstick — Coloring pen — Loop forming mandrel — Paint brush

forms made from PVC designed specifically for nylon flower making.

Q Where to find materials and tools for nylon flowers?

A Nylon flower making is just being re-introduced in the United States. There are very few craft stores in the U.S. that currently carry nylon flower materials. For more information on the materials and tools please go to www.newsheer.com

Q What steps are involved in making nylon flowers?

A The basic steps for making nylon flowers are: 1) make a wire loop, 2) wrap wire loop with nylon, 3) shape loops into petals or leaves, 4) attach flower and leaves to stem, and 5) arrange flowers and leaves.

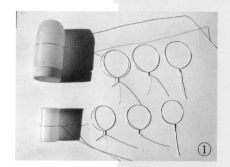

Make Wire Loop Tightly wrap wire around circular form, and then twist the two ends of the wire together 4-5 times to close the loop. Keep one end of the wire at least 1-inch long to create a handle for the loop. The handle is used to attach petals or leaves together. Some flowers require long handle as specified in the instructions. Use flat-nose pliers to flatten down any wire end that is sticking out (Photo 1).

Wrap Nylon Wrap the loop inside the nylon and then use nylon or cotton thread to cinch the nylon at the loop handle. Trim off excess nylon with scissors (Photo 2).

Shape Petal and Leaf Once the loop has been covered in nylon, use your

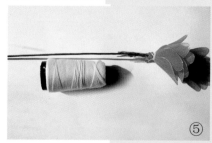

thumb, forefinger and middle finger from both hands to shape loop into the petal or leaf according to the type of flower. While some circumstances may require you to shape the loop before it has been covered with the nylon, normally the shaping is done after loop has been covered(Photo 3).

Assemble Flower and Leaf Depending on the type of flower, several petals are tied together to form the flower. When assembling flowers, pay attention to its form, the shape of the stamen, whether the flower has a stem and if so, the stem's length. After the flower has been assembled, trim off excess wire at the base of the flower (near the stem). To make the flower stem as smooth as possible, use flat-nose pliers to flatten down any wire ends that may be sticking out (Photos 4, 5).

Wrap tape and Final Touches For most flowers, the stem needs to be wrapped with floral tape. The tape not only water proofs the stem, it also gives the flower a more realistic look. Different color tapes can be applied depending on the type of flower (Photo 6). Once the flower has been assembled, spend time to shape the flower and adjust the petals to create a more natural look. Note some flower stems also have unique shapes and characteristics.

Q What are some of the special techniques used in this book?

A Some of the flowers and leaves in this book employ non-traditional methods. Below are some examples of these special techniques:

1. Using a bottle brush method to make flowers – Cut nylon into strips, twist the wires to pinch and secure the nylon strips. This method is used for baby's breath, wood forget-me-not, and crepe-myrtle.

2. Using Styrofoam balls to create flowers with unique shapes – String of Pearls, Crepe-myrtle, Chinese Lantern Flower, etc.

3. Using cotton and white glue to make buds for Freesia, Agapanthus, Bulrush, etc.

4. Combining paper and glue with nylon to achieve unique looks – Rosary Vine, Cattail and Ivy.

5. Folding loops into appropriate shapes after the wire loops have been wrapped with nylon, such as Bird of Paradise and Heliconia.

6. Leveraging acrylic paint or ink to enhance petals and leaves and make them look more realistic. Some petals and leaves have dramatic color contrasts in nature. Paint can help create the contrast that nylon alone can not.

7. Making stamens and pistils. Flowers can have very different shape, size and colored stamens and pistils. Ready-made stamens and pistils are mostly matchstick or button shaped which are not suitable for many flowers. Self-made stamens and pistils add a level of detail to nylon flowers that is necessary to achieve the best results.

Q How do I make stamens and pistils?

A Sunflowers, Blue Star, Narcissus, Egyptian Blue Lily, among others, have stamens that require special techniques. Refer to the instructional page for each flower for more details. Below is a brief description of a commonly used method for stamen/pistil making.

Making string-style stamen: a commonly used method for stamen/pistil making. Take white and yellow cotton or nylon thread and wet with glue. After the glue dries, cut the thread to required length (usually about 1 ½-inch long). Use a hot iron or glue to attach small grains to the thread to create speckles on the stamens. This type of stamen can be found in Clematis, Gladiolus, Freesia, etc.

Q How do I make buds look as realistic as possible?

A When making nylon flowers, buds are a component that should

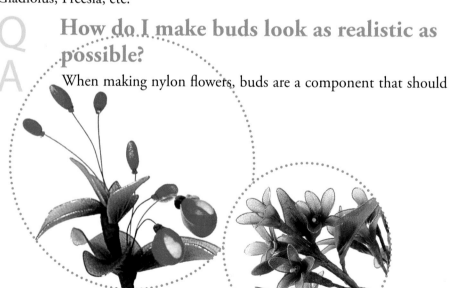

not be overlooked. Some plants have very attractive buds, such as Kaido Crab Apple, Agapanthus, Freesia, and Blue Star. Note the color transition from bud, to half-open flower, to flower in full bloom. The bud can not be simply wrapped in green nylon, or the exact color of the blooming flower, becasue its color can contain hints of both shades. Kaido Crab Apple plant is at the peak of its beauty just before it blooms. To make Kaido Crab Apple buds, wrap green nylon around scrap pieces of nylon the same color as the flower. When making Freesia, to show different levels of maturity, some buds are created using green nylon; some are wrapped with a layer of same color nylon as the flower. Finally an outer layer of green nylon is added; the rest are the same color as the flower.

Q How do I make flowers look as realistic as possible without wasting materials?

A There are close to a hundred nylon colors available on the market, including both single and dual-colors. But in nature, flowers can take on endless colors. The petals of a flower can vary in shade. Some flowers, such as Gladiolus, have petals that are darker in the middle and lighter in the outer layers. Roses, on the other hand, can have lighter middle, darker outside, or vice versa. In some cases, the inner and outer layers may be different shades. Don't be too sparing when using different color nylons in one flower. They are sometimes necessary to achieve the desired results. Save leftover nylon scraps as they may be useful for making other flowers. For example, Baby's Breath and Blazing-star can be made from scrap nylon pieces.

Chinese Rose

Rosa chinensis, known commonly as Chinese Rose, belongs to the Rosaceae family, the same family as the common rose. China Rose has a similar shape to common roses, but the thorns have hooks.

Many China Rose varieties can be recreated as nylon flowers. Note that due to the limitation of nylon that's currently on the market, nylon flowers can not match the true color and vibrance of fresh flowers.

「Materials」

#24 wire, #24 green wire.

Thick and thin stem wire.

Nylon fabric in white, cream, yellow, peach, light pink, pink, fuchsia, blue and various shades of red and green.

Green floral tape, cotton balls, white glue, nylon or cotton thread.

「Instructions」

Making the Loops: Use #24 wire to make the following size loops: five 1 ¼-inch diameter loops, six 1 ¼-inch-diameter loops, and seven 2-inch diameter loops. The number and size of loops can be adjusted based on desired flower size.

Trim off any excess wire from the loop. Use flat pliers to flatten the twisted section in order to remove sharp points (Picture 1).

Petals: Select a nylon fabric of desired color, roll up the fabric (like rolling up a nylon sock) and cut off a piece to get a small sheet. Wrap the nylon around a loop and use nylon thread to tie off the nylon. Trim off any excess nylon. Form each petal into a fan shape. Pinch 4-5 waves in the small petal, 2-3 waves in medium and large petals. Then curl the lower part of each wave inward slightly.

Stamen: Select a thick flower stem wire. Add a few drops of glue to a thumb-sized piece of cloth, then use this cloth to wipe some glue onto one end of the rod, covering about one inch. Wrap a cotton ball around the wire like a Q-Tip (Picture 2).

Take small pieces of nylon fabric, stack them, and wrap them around the cotton ball. Then cut a

2½ x 5-inch rectangular piece of nylon fabric, fold in half along the long edge, and spiral this strip around the Q-tip, keeping the folded edge toward the top of the flower. This forms the stamen (Picture 3).

Assembly: Tie fie small flower petals around the stamen using nylon thread. Then tie six more medium-sized petals around the small petals. Finally, tie seven large flower petals around the outside (Picture 4). Trim any excess wire. Take care to trim the wires from different petals to different lengths, rather than all the same length; this results in a smoother layering on the stem. Tightly wrap green tape around the flower stem, covering the petal wires smoothly.

Leaves: Make several 1-inch, 1 ¼-inch, and 1 ½-inch diameter wire loops. Wrap green nylon around the loops, then shape the loops into rose leaves.

Cut 4- to 6-inch long rods from #20 green wire to make leaf stems. Use green floral tape to attach one small leaf to each rod. Then attach two medium or large leaves symmetrically around the rod. Repeat to make several 3-leaf or 5-leaf stems. Arrange the leaf stems around the flower stem; wrap green floral tape aound the stems (Picture 5).

Tulip

「Materials」

#24 silver wires.

Thick stem wire.

White, red, pink, yellow, orange nylons
(you can also use dual-color nylon).

Light green floral tape.

「Instructions」

Petals:

Each tulip has six petals. Use silver wire
to make six 2 ¼ to 2 ½-inch loops. Wrap
nylon around each loop and then pinch the
loop into an oval shape. (Picture 1).

Assembly:

Wrap floral tape around the stem wire
several times, starting from one end to
cover about 1¼-inch of the wire. Tie the six
petals around the stem wire with the petals
upside down, forming two layers of petals
(Picture 2). Cut off excess wires and then
flip the petals around towards the tip of the
wire. Arrange the petals and bend the tip of
each petal inward slightly (Picture 3).

Trout Lily

⌈Materials⌋
#24 silver wire.
#20 green wire.
Purple, lavender nylons.
and green.

⌈Instructions⌋

Petals and Leaves:

Use #24 silver wire to make two 1 ½-inch diameter loops. Wrap green nylon around the loops and pinch loops into the shape a of long, thin leaf (Picture 1). Use #24 silver wire to make six 1 1/4-inch loops. Wrap purple and lavender nylon around the loops, pinch the loops into tongue-shapes with a thin tip (Picture 2).

Assembly:

Cut #20 green wire into desired length for the stem and wrap in green floral tape. Tie six petals upside down around one end of wire with three petals per layer in two layers (Picture 3). Flip the petals around towards the tip of the wire and arrange them (Picture 4). Attach two leaves on the wire at least 5 ½-inch away from the flower. The 2 leaves should be at the same level. Use tape to attach the leaves and continue to tape all the way to the end of the wire (Picture 5).

Final Touch:
Bend the rod, starting at about ¾-inch from the flower, so that the flower droops downward.

13

Poppies

「Materials」

#24 silver wire.

Thin stem wire.

White, pale yellow, yellow, red, peach, pink, purple or dual-color nylons.

Light green floral tape.

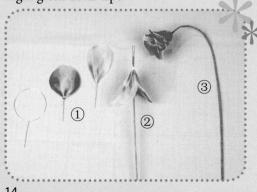

「Instructions」

Petals: Each poppy has six petals. Use silver wire to make six 2¼-inch diameter loops and wrap loops with nylon of desired color (see Picture 1).

Assembly: Cover entire rod with a layer of floral tape and then wrap one end of the wire again ⅜ to ½-inch long. Tie the petals upside down to the wire upside down (similar to Tulip on Page 12). Stagger three petals around double-taped end of stem wire and tape the petals to rod. Arrange the remaining three petals outside of other three petals and tape to wire (Picture 2). Trim excess wire to leave a stub. Cover stub in with more floral tape. Flip petals over and shape each petal to form 2-3 waves.

Final Touch: bend the rod, starting at about 1 ½-2-inch from the flower, so that the flower droops downward.

Sweet Pea

「Materials」

#24 silver wire.

#18 green wire.

Thin stem wire.

White, pink, peach, red, lavender or dual-color nylons.

Light green floral tape.

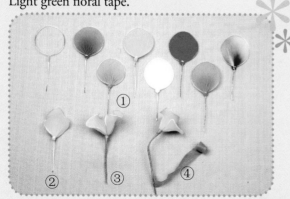

「Instructions」

Petals: Use silver wire to make desired quantity of 1½ -inch diameter loops (Picture 1), leaving a 1¼ to 1½-inch handle on each loop. Each flower has two petals and each branch has 4-5 flowers. Wrap nylon around loop and then bend the petal to make it wavy (Picture 2)

Assembly: Twist the handles of two petals together and cover with floral tape (Picture 3).Cut #18 green wire to 12 to 15 inches long. Attach four or five flowers to the wire with green tape, and bend the wire slightly to give it a natural curve (Picture 4).

Bauhinia

[Materials]

#24 silver wire.

Thin stem wire (13.5-inch long).

Magenta color nylon.

Red and green floral tape.

Ready-made stamen for calla lily (1 light green and 5 white stamens per flower) or make stamen using air-dry clay.

White or green acrylic paint.

[Instructions]

Petals:

(1) Five petals per flower. Use silver wire to make five 2¼-inch diameter loops, leaving a 1¼-inch long handle on each loop (Picture 1).

(2) Wrap nylon around the loops and then using a thin paint brush and white paint, draw thin lines to form a leaf vein pattern. Form 3-4 waves into the petal and then stretch the petal to elongate it (Pictures 2, 3).

(3) Wrap the base of the flower with red floral tape.

Stamen:

Use air-dry clay to make the filaments that form the stamen. Mix with white or green coloring to make white or light green stamens. Roll the clay into pistil or sprout form (Picture 4).

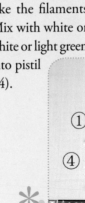

Sunflower

[Materials]

#24 silver wire.

Thick stem wire.

Yellow color nylon.

Green floral tape.

Coffee and mustard colored thick yarn.

[Instructions]

Petals: Use wire to make twenty-four 1 ½-inch diameter loops. Wrap nylon around the loops and then form loops into long, oval shapes.

Stamen: Use thin knitting needles to knit a circular shaped patch, coffee colored with mustard yellow highlights (Picture 2).

Assembly: (1) Select thick wire. Tie 10 petals around one end of the rod with thread. Trim off excess wire (Picture 3). Tie remaining 14 petals on the outside of the initial 10 petals. Again, trim off excess wire. Flatten wire ends with flat-nose pliers.

(2) Open up the flower petals, and sew knitted stamen to the middle of the flower (you can use a regular sewing needle). Finally wrap green floral tape around the rod to form a stem (Picture 4).

Sydney Flannel Flower

⌈Instructions⌋

Petals: Each flower takes 11-12 petals. Make 11-12 loops in 1 ½ inch diameter with #24 silver wire. Cover loop with nylon (Picture 1). If the nylon is too thin, add another layer of nylon. Form loops into olive shapes (Picture 2).

Assembly: Bend #20 green wire into a U-shape and thread the button-shaped stamen through one end until the stamen is at the bottom of the U (picture3) Crimp two-halves of the wires together. Tie petals around the stamen and trim excess wires for petals. Wrap the entire length of the stem with green floral tape.

Arrange the petals into a flower shape. Use green paint to tint tip of each petal lightly.

⌈Materials⌋

#24 silver wire.
#20 green wire.
White nylon.
Green floral tape.
Ready-made stamen in the shape of button in grassy green color (optional: do-it-yourself – use mossy green yarn to crochet or knit the stamen)

Each flower takes 12-15 petals

Marguerite

⌈Materials⌋

#24 silver wire, #20 green wire.
White nylon.
Orange colored, ready-made stamen in the shape of a button.
Light green floral tape.

⌈Instructions⌋

Petals: Each flower takes 12-15 petals. Make 12-15 loops in 1 1/4-inch diameter with #24 silver wire. Cover each loop with nylon. Form loops into thin, long oval shapes.

Stamen: Bend #20 green wire into a U-shape, and thread the button-shaped stamen through one end until the stamen is at the bottom of the U. Crimp two-halves of the wire together.

Assembly: Tie petals around the stamen and trim excess wire. Wrap the entire length of the stem with green floral tape. Arrange the petals.

19

Daffodil

⌈Materials⌋

#24 silver and gold wires.
#18 green wire (12-inch long).
Pale yellow and yellow nylon.
1 ½-inch string stamen (see Page 8 for instructions).
Light green floral tape.

⌈Instructions⌋

Petals: Use silver wire to make six 1¼-inch diameter loops and wrap them with pale yellow nylon. Form loops into almond shapes (Picture 1).

Make three 3/4-inch diameter loops and cover with yellow nylon and gold wire. Form loops into fan shapes (Picture 2). Pinch 2-3 waves into the fan shape.

Assembly: Tie six string stamens to the #18 green wire. Arrange fan-shaped yellow petals around the stamen (Picture 3). Stagger the six pale yellow petals around the yellow petals with three petals per layer in two layers (Picture 4). Trim excess wire and cover entire length of green wire with floral tape.

②
③
①
④

Japanese Iris

⌈Materials⌋

#24 silver wire

Thin stem wire (12-inch long).

Purple, lavender and green nylon

Green floral tape

⌈Instructions⌋

Petals: Each flower has six petals. Make three 1 ¼-inch diameter loops and three 2-inch loops with silver wire. Cover larger loops with purple nylon and pinch 4-5 waves into each loop. Cover smaller loops in lavender nylon and pinch 3-4 waves into each loop (Pictures 1,2).

Leaves: Make two 2 ¼-inch diameter loops and cover with green nylon. Form loops into leaf shapes. Crease the leaf in the middle length-wise (Picture 3,4).

Assembly: Tie the 3 smaller petals to one end of the stem wire. Stagger the three larger petals outside of the smaller leaves. Trim off excess wires. Attach the first leaf about 1½-inch from the bottom of the flower, then attach the 2nd leaf at 1½-inch from the 1st leaf (Picture 5).

Final Touch: Pull up the three petals at the center to elongate them and make them stand upwards. Open up the three larger purple petals with an upward tilt. Wrap the first leaf tightly around the stem to create the look of unopened leaf. Wrap the second leaf around the stem and first leaf.

Egyptian Blue Lily

⌈Materials⌋
#24 silver wire.
Thin stem wire (11 ¾-inch long)
Blue-violet, purple and yellow nylon
Brown floral tape.
White glue (slightly diluted with water)

⌈Instruction⌋

Petals: Make 17 loops with the silver wire, 1½-inch diameter each. Keep a ¾-inch handle on each loop. Wrap wires with blue-violet nylon and then form loops into a long, oval shape (Picture 1).

Stamen: Glue two layers of purple nylon together (you can use scraps). After the glue dries, cut about 40 strips, 2-inch long. Repeat with yellow nylon to make about 30 strips (Picture 2).

Assembly: Tie yellow stamen strip to the end of stem wire. Then surround yellow strips with purple strips to create the stamen. Arrange eight petals around the stamen and then stagger nine petals on the outside (Picture 3). Cover stem with brown floral tape.

Final Touch: Keep the petals upward slightly to create a half-open look. Having the flowers in the bouquet at different stages of bloom creates a more realistic look.

Shannon Water Lily

⌈Materials⌋

#24 silver wire.

#20 green wire.

Pale yellow, golden yellow and green nylon.

Orange colored, ready-made stamen in the shape of a button. (see Page 22 Egyptian Water Lily for instruction).

⌈Instructions⌋

Petals and leaves:

Using silver wire, make seven loops, 1¼-inch diameter each and 23 loops with a 1¾ diameter. Keep a 1 ½-inch handle on each loop. Wrap seven small and seven large loops with golden yellow nylon. Form loops into long, olive shape (Picture 1).

Wrap 11 of the large loops in pale yellow nylon. Form loops into long, oval shapes (Picture 2).

Wrap remaining five large loops in green nylon and form them into leaf shapes (Picture 3).

Assembly: Thread the #20 green wire through the button stamen (see Sydney Flannel Flower on Page 18). Layer the petals and leaves.

Final Touch: Spread petals and leaves.

Dahlia

「Materials」
#24 silver wire.
Thin stem wire.
Red, yellow, pink, fuchsia
color nylon and dual-color nylon
Thick nylon thread
Green floral tape

「Instructions」

Petals: Using silver wire, make 20 loops, 1⅓-inch diameter each (large) and 20 loops in 1½ diameter (small). Wrap loops in desired color, note that the color is lighter at the tip of the petal (Picture 1).

Form the large petals into tongue shape with a pointed tip (Picture 2).

Stretch and elongate 10 small petals and twist one end to form a slight spiral. (Picture 3).

Take the remaining 10 small petals, stretch and elongate and then twist them slightly (Picture 4).

Assembly: Cover one end of the stem wire several times with tape. Tie 10 spiral shaped petals to the stem using thick nylon thread. Arrange and tie the other 10 small petals. Finally, layer and tie the 20 large petals. Trim off excess wire. Wrap stem wire with tape.

①
②
③
④

Chinese Peony

⌈Materials⌋
#24 silver wire.
Thin stem wire.
Green, pink, fuchsia, orange nylon.
Green floral tape.

⌈Instruction⌋

Petals: Each flower has 12 petals. Use silver wire to make six loops, 1½-inch diameter each and six loops in 2-inch diameter. Keep a 1-inch handle on each loop.
Use pink or fuchsia nylon to wrap the loops and then form them into fan shapes (Picture 1).

Leaves: Make five 1-inch loops. Use green nylon to wrap the loops and then form them into leaf shapes.

Stamen: Take scrap nylon in orange or other dual-colors (use curly material for best results), then cut 2-inch long, ½ to ¾-inch wide strips (Picture 2).

Assembly: Cover one end of the stem wire several times with tape. Tie 15-20 strips of orange stamen to the stem wire. Arrange 6 smaller petals around the stamen, then surround the flower with the larger petals. Trim off excess wire (Picture 3).

Final Touch: Use the green leaves to cover up the bulge, and wrap entire stem with floral tape.

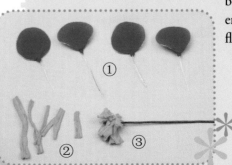

① ② ③

25

Moluccella

⌈Materials⌋

#22 silver wire.
Thin stem wire.
Apple green nylon.
Light green floral tape.
White match stick shaped stamen
(ready-made).

⌈Instructions⌋

Petals: Use silver wire to make 24 loops,
1 ¾-inch diameter each; 12 loops
in 1 ¼-inch diameter, 18 loops in
1 1/3-inch diameter, eight loops in
1-inch diameter, and six loops in
¾-inch diameter. Wrap all loops in
green nylon (Picture 1).

Form loops into a fan shapes. Use a
knitting needle to curl the bottom of
the petals, put a stamen inside and then
further tighten the curl (Picture 2).

Assembly: Attach petals to stem wire using
floral tape. Form clusters with 4-6
petals and space clusters 1 ¼ to
2-inch apart. Sequence the petals
so that the smallest petals are on top
of the rod and the largest are on the
bottom.

①

②

Blue Star

⌈Materials⌋

#20 and #30 green wire.

#24 and #26 silver wire.

Sky blue, green, pale green or similar dual-color nylons.

White match stick shaped stamen (ready-made).

Green floral tape, cotton ball, white glue.

⌈Instructions⌋

Petals: Use #26 silver wire to make ¾-inch diameter loops in desired quantity (five petals per flower). Keep a 1 ¼ - 1 ½-inch handle on the loop. Cover loops with sky blue nylon and then stretch them into long strips (Picture 1).

Bud: Glue a cotton ball to the tip of #30 green wire (2-inch long). Form the cotton ball into an olive shape. Cover cotton with green nylon and then wrap wire with green tape (Picture 2).

Stamen: Apply glue to stamen and wrap a small piece of sky blue nylon around stamen; Apply glue again and cover sky blue stamen with green nylon. Be sure to leave the tip of the match stick stamen exposed, showing a little white color (Picture 3).

Leaves: Use #24 silver wire to make loops with a 1 to 1 ¼-inch diameter; cover loops with green nylon and form loops into cone shapes. Wrap handle and base of leaf with green floral tape.

Assembly: Form a flower with five petals and one stamen. Take a 14-inch #20 green wire and tie 3-5 flowers and 1-2 buds to the wire with green floral tape to create a branch (Picture 5).

Dendrobium Orchid

⌈Materials⌋

#24 and #26 silver wire.

Thick stem wire.

Nylon fabric: white, yellow and pale yellow (you can also use a green and pale green combination).

Light green and green floral tape.

⌈Instructions⌋

Stamen: Use #26 silver wire to make a ½ inch diameter loop. Cover the loop with yellow nylon and then form loop into a tongue shape (Picture 1).

Sepal: Use #26 silver wire to make one 1½-inch loop. Cover loop with pale yellow nylon and then form loop into a fan shape. Pinch the edge of the loop to create waves and then curl the loop into a cone shape (Picture 2).

Petal: Make three 1½-inch diameter loops and two 1-inch diameter loops using #24 silver wire. Keep a 2-inch long handle on the loops. Cover loops with white nylon and form them into an oval shape (Picture 3).

Assembly: Tie the stamen and the sepal together with thread. Attach two petals (1-inch) on the outside. Finally, form the outer-most layer with the remaining three large petals. Trim off excess wire and then use light green tape to wrap the handles (Picture 4).

Flowering Maple

⌈Materials⌋

#24 silver wire.
Thin stem wire.
Powder pink nylon.
Light green floral tape.
Purple paint.

⌈Instructions⌋

Each branch has 9 flowers and each flower requires five petals and one sepal.

Petals: (1) Make 54 loops, each 1-inch in diameter with a ¾-inch handle. Wrap loops with nylon (Picture 1).

(2) Take nine loops and form these into a tongue shape. Pinch a small tail just above the handle. Draw tiny dots using a small paint brush and purple paint. These nine loops are now the sepals (Picture 2).

(3) Form the other 45 loops into almond shapes.

Assembly:

(1) To make one flower, tie together five petals and one sepal. The sepal is in the middle. The petals are staggered to form two layers, with two petals in the inner layer and three in the outer. Trim off excess wire, but leave 1–2 wires handles, wrapping them in light green floral tape (Picture 3).

(2) Attach a flower to the tip of the stem wire using green tape and keep 1¼-inch long stem. Tape remaining flowers around the stem. Each flower should be slightly offset. Space the flowers about 1½-inch apart (Picture 4).

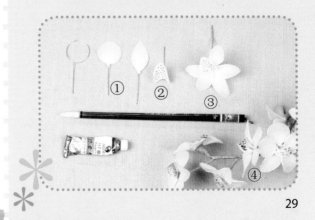

Boat Orchid

⌜Instructions⌟

Petal: (1) Make 42 loops, each 1¼-inch in diameter with a 2–inch handle. Wrap loops with nylon, if you are using dual-color fabric, note the direction of the color bands (Picture 1).

(2) Take seven loops and form them into fan shape. Pinch 2–3 waves into each loop, and bend the tip of the loop downward (Picture 2). These are the sepals.

(3) Form 21 of the remaining loops into long, thin tongue shapes (Picture 3) and form the remaining 14 loops into short tongue shapes (Picture 4).

Assembly: (1) Tie two short tongue-shaped petals to one sepal. Layer three long tongue-shaped petals on the outside. The petals should be staggered, with the sepal at the bottom. Trim off excess wires, leaving one or two wires untouched as the stem for the flower. Wrap the stem with green tape. Repeat step (1) for remaining six flowers (Picture 4).

(2) Attach a flower to the tip of the stem wire using a green tape keeping ¾-inch long stem. Tape the second flower about 2 ½-inch from the first flower. Remaining flowers should be attached about 1⅓-inch apart. Cover the entire stem wire with tape (Picture 5).

Final Touch: Arrange the three long petals to form a "Y". The sepal should be at the bottom of the middle section.

⌜Materials⌟

#24 silver wire.
Thin stem wire.
Purple and white(dual-color nylon is ideal).
Green floral tape.

Each branch has seven flowers. Each flower requires five petals and one sepal.

Parrots Beak

⌜Materials⌟

#24 silver wire.
#20 gold wire.
Thick stem wire.
Orange, orange-red, coral nylons.
Light green floral tape.
White glue.

⌜Instructions⌟

(1) Using the silver wire, make one 3-inch, one 2½-inch, and one 1 ½-inch diameter loops, one each (Picture 1). Wrap the largest loop with orange nylon. Wrap the two smaller loops in orange-red nylon (Picture 2).

Fold the loops in half and pull to elongate. Take one 2 ½-inch long gold wire and cover in white glue. Roll a small piece of orange colored nylon around the wire to make the stamen.

Tape two orange-red loops and the stamen to the top of the stem wire keeping the stamen in the middle. Attach the orange loop about ½-inch below the other loops. Wrap the rest of the stem wire with tape (Picture 3).

(2) Using the silver wire, make two 3-inch diameter loops, two 2 ¼-inch diameter loop, and one 1½-inch diameter loop. Follow step 1 to make petals and stamen.
Tape two petals and the stamen to the top of the stem wire. Continue to wrap the stem wire. Attach at 4¾-inch mark, attach 2 more petals. Wrap the rest of the stem wire with tape.

① ② ③

Heliconia

⌈Materials⌋

#24 silver wire.
#18 green wire (or thin stem wire).
Red or orange nylons.
Red and green floral tape.
Red and yellow acrylic paint.

⌈Instructions⌋

Petal: Using #24 silver wire, make two 1¼ -inch diameter loops, three 2-inch diameter loops, and four 2¼-inch diameter loops. Wrap with red or orange nylon (each stalk must have the same color petals). Form each petal into a peach shape and then fold in half.

Assembly: Attach two small petals to the top of the stem wire using red floral tape, nesting one petal inside the other. Add a medium-sized petal about ½-inch below. Attach the remaining petals first with medium petals, then with large petals, ¾-inch apart, alternating sides. After all petals have been attached, wrap the rest of the stem wire with green tape.

Final Touch: Wrap every petal tightly around the stem. Each petal should hug the base of the petal above. Create a curve in the stem wire between every pair of petals. Use paint to tint the edge of each petal. Use yellow paint on red nylon and red paint on orange nylon.

Brake Fern

⌈Materials⌋

#18 and #22 green wire.
Grassy green nylon.
Light green floral tape.
Dark green acrylic paint.

⌈Instructions⌋

Leaf:

Each frond of the brake fern requires three or five leaves. Using #22 green wire, make desired quantity of 2 ¼, 3, and 4 -inch diameter loops. Keep a 1 ½" length handle on each loop.

Wrap loops in green nylon and then form them into an olive shape. Pinch a few waves along both sides of the leaf, then flatten the leaf. Cover the handle of the leaf with light green tape. Tint the edge of the leaf with dark green paint.

Assembly:

Tie three to five leaves to #18 green wire with tape. Another way to make a three-leaf frond is to tie together a pair of smaller leaves and one larger leaf, with the larger leaf in the middle. Attach the frond to the stem on #18 green wire.

33

Baby's Breath

⌈Materials⌋

#20 and #30 light green wire.

White and light green nylon.

⌈Instructions⌋

Flower: (1) Cut #30 wire to about 4¾-inch long. Bend one end of the wire to make a ½-inch hook. Cut white nylon to ⅛ x ¾-inch strips. Scraps from other projects can be used (photo 1).

(2) Drape a few strips of nylon on the hook and twist the hook closed to create a tight loop that locks the nylon strips inside (photo 2).

(3) Cut off excess wire (shorter end only). Remove any loose nylon strips that are not secured. Trim the height of nylon strips to about ½-inch. Fluff the flower to create a velvety texture (photos 3,4).

(4) To make a bud, repeat steps (1) through (4) using green nylon, but trim the final height of the nylon strip (flower) to about ⅜-inch (photo 5).

Assembly: Twist white flowers and green buds together to create an umbrella-shaped stalk.

(1) Twist the wires of two white flowers together to form a lopsided Y, leaving one wire about ¾-inch longer than the other at the bottom (photo 6).

(2) To add the third flower, twist its wire with the extra ¾-inch wire from the lopsided Y. There should be one extra inch of wire at the bottom. Repeat to attach another seven flowers/buds (about 10 total). The bottom wire should be about 1¼ to 2-inch long at this point (photos 8,9).

(3) Cut #20 green wire to 12-inch long. Attach three stalks of flowers to the top half of the #20 green wire, leaving a section about 4 to 6-inch long at the bottom.

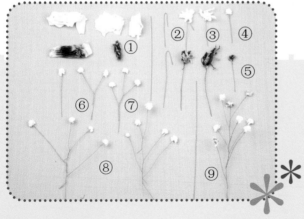

34

Baby's Breath

Lily

Asiatic lilies come in a multitude of vibrant colors. Each stalk has four to five flowers.

The Casa Blanca Oriental Lily comes in white or pink and is pleasantly fragrant. Each stalk has two to three flowers.

The Easter Lily is white. The flower is horn shaped and tilts sideways or slightly down. It does not open up completely, even in full bloom. Each stalk has only one or two flowers.

⌈Materials⌋

Thin stem wire.
#24 green or white wire.
#24 silver wire.
Green, light green, white, yellow, peach-red, powder pink nylon.
Ready-made plastic stamen.
Green or white nylon thread.
Green floral tape.

Asiatic Lily

Easter Lily

Casa Blanca
Oriental Lily

⌈Instructions⌋

Bud: Take 2 ¼ to 3-inch form, wrap #24 green or white wire around the form three times. Using a small piece of wire tie together loops then twist the small piece of wire and end wires a few times to tie off the loops, then cut off the shorter end of the wire. Tighten the knot with pliers (photo 1). Tie the top of the three loops together with nylon thread. Stretch the loops to elongate, then space out of the loops evenly to create a three dimensional shape similar to a jalapeno pepper (see photo 2). Cover the smaller buds with green nylon and bigger buds with white nylon. Cover the stalk/stem with green tape (photo 3).

Petal: Each lily has six petals of equal size. Take #24 silver wire to make 2 ½ to 3-inch diameter loops (keeping 2 ¼-inch handle). Depending on the lily variety, select the appropriate color nylon to cover the loops (photo 4).

Stamen: Each lily stamen has seven filaments. They are light yellow, light green or red. They can be made from air-dry clay or may be purchased (photo 5).

Assembly: (1) Tie together six petals with nylon thread – three petals per layer with a stamen in the middle. Trim off any excess wire and wrap the stem with green tape.

Polianthes Tuberosa

「Materials」

#26 silver wire.

#22 and #24 wire (1¼ to 1½-inch long sections, you can use scrap wire).

Thick stem wire.

White and pale green nylon

Light green floral tape.

White and white string stamens, 1½-inch long (see Page 8 for instructions).

Cotton ball, white glue.

「Instructions」

Makes three blooming flowers (six petals per flower) and one partially open flower (four petals per flower).

Petal: (1) Take #26 silver wire and make 22 loops with a 1-inch diameter (photo 1). Wrap loops in white nylon, then form into an olive shape (photo 2).

(2) Tie three petals around the stamen using four white stamens and one yellow stamen. Stagger another three petals around the outside. Wrap the stem with light green tape.

(3) Repeat step (2) with four petals to make a half-open flower. (photo 3).

Bud: Take a 1¼-inch wire section and make a little hook on one end. Dip hook in white glue and then attach a cotton ball. Form the cotton into an olive shape. Make 30 buds in equal quantities with three different sizes (small, medium and large) (photo 3). Cover the small buds with pale green nylon and the remaining buds with white nylon. Trim off excess wires. For the medium and large buds, cover the handle with green tape.

Assembly: Attach four to five small buds to the top of the stem wire with green tape (photo 4). Continue to attach buds around the stem wire until all buds are used. Then attach a half-open flower and finally the full bloomed flowers. Wrap remaining stem wire in green tape.

Final Touch: Arrange all buds so they stand straight up, close to the stem wire. For the half-open flower, bend the tips of the four petals outward slightly. For the full-flower, bend three of the six petals outward.

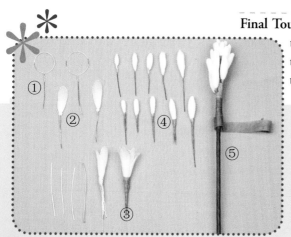

Polianthes Tuberosa

Each Polianthes tuberosa stalk has more than 30 buds. The flowers start to bloom from the bottom of the stalk up. When in full bloom, petals open upward.

Iris

「Materials」

#24 silver wire.
Either thick or thin stem wire (11¾-inch long).
Nylon fabric: purple, lavender, green.
Green floral tape.
Orange acrylic paint.

「Instructions」

Petal: (1) Using #24 silver wire, make nine 2-inch diameter loops (six for the flowers, three for the buds). Cover six loops with lavender nylon (photo 1), three with purple nylon (photo 2).

2) Paint a peanut (both size and shape) on three lavender loops (photo 3). Once the paint dries, pinch 3-4 waves into the edge of the loop. These are the outer petals (photo 4). Form the three inner purple petals into long, olive shape and pinch 5-6 waves to the sides of the petals (photo 5). Tie these six petals to the end of the stem wire.

(3) Take the three remaining lavender loops and form them into long, olive shape (photo 6). Tie the petals to the end of a stem wire, with one petal in the middle and two petals on the outside. Wrap the petals tightly around each other.

Leaf: Make seven 2¼-inch diameter loops with #24 silver wire (three for the flowers, four for the buds) (photo 9). Cover loops with green nylon, form them into leaf shape, then fold the leaf in half (photo 10).

Assembly: (1) Take the stem wire with the flower attached and continue to wrap with green tape. Attach a leaf about an inch below the flower. Wrap tape around another inch, attach another leaf. Attach the third leaf in similar fashion, then cover the rest of the stem wire with green tape (photo 11).

(2) Take the stem wire with bud attached, wrap two leaves just below the bud such that the leaves can almost cover up the bud completely. Then at 2-inch intervals, attach the third leaf and fourth leaf. Cover the rest of the stem wire with green tape (photo 12).

Final Touch: Open the petals with orange painted outward to open up the flowers. Arrange the inner three petals tightly around each other and keep them upright. The three leaves should hug the stem. For the bud, also keep the petals wrap tightly around each other and upright; the four leaves should hug the stem, with the upper two leaves wrapped tightly to the bottom of the flower.

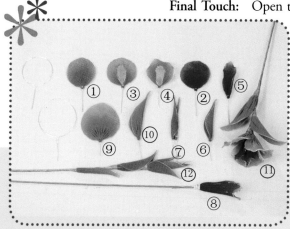

Iris

Freesia

⌈Materials⌋

#24 silver wire, #20 and #22 green wire.
Green, white, yellow, red, lavender,
peach-red, etc. nylon.
Green floral tape.
Cotton ball, white glue.

⌈Instructions⌋

Bud: Use #22 green wire, cotton ball and white glue
to make buds. Form cotton ball into almond
shape of various sizes. Cover small buds with
green nylon; cover large buds with the same color nylon as the flower,
then again cover with green nylon (photo 1).

Petal: Use #24 silver wire to make 15 loops at 1 ½-inch diameter (these make
two blooming flowers and one partially blooming flower), maintain
about 1 ½" long handle on the loop. Cover loops with nylon of desired
colors. Wrap handle with green tape (photo 2).

Stamen: Freesias have string stamen, four filaments per flower. Make string style
stamen using thick nylon thread. (see page 8)

Assembly: (1) Tie stamen and three petals together. Attach another three petals
on the outside. Trim off excess wire. Wrap handles with green tape.
(2) Partially blooming flower requires only three petals. Stamen is still
invisible at this point and can be skipped. Tie three petals together, trim
off excess wire, and wrap handle with green tape (photo 3)
(3) Use #20 green wire as stem. Tie the smallest bud to the tip of the stem
with green tape (photo 4). Continue to attach buds to the same side of
the stem, from smallest to largest.
(4) Once all the flowers and buds have been
attached, fold the remaining stem in half,
wrap remaining stem with green tape. Curve
the stem just below the bottom flower.

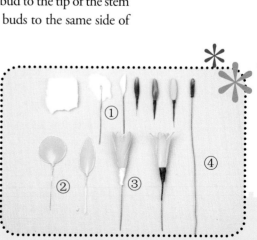

Freesia

Freesia flowers have six petals. Each stalk can hold as many as 10 flowers and buds. Freesias are at its most attractive when the stalk has both blooming flowers and buds.

Eustoma

「Materials」

#24 silver wire.

#20 green wire (2 ¾-inch, 4-inch, one each).

Thin stem wire (11¾-inch).

White, pink, purple, green nylons or dual-color in similar shades.

Green floral tape.

Stamen: see Page 16 for instructions to make 3 stamens and 15 pistils

「Instructions」

Eustoma flowers are horn shaped, with five petals per flower. The instructions below make a stalk with three flowers and one bud with six leaves.

Petal: Use #24 silver wire to make 15 loops in 1¼-inch with 2-inch handles. Cover loops with nylon in desired colors. Form loops into peach shape (Photo 1). Tie five petals together, with one stamen and five pistils in the center (Photo 2). Trim off all excess wires except 1-2 strands then wrap with green tape (Photo 3).

Bud: Loop #24 silver wire around ¾-inch form 3 times. Twist the two end wires together to close off the loops. Trim off one end and leave 2-inch on the other end of the wire. Use thread to tie the three loops together at the top. Pinch the loops into long oval shape (Photo 4).

Leaf: Use #24 silver wire to make six 1½-inch loops. Cover loops with green nylon then shape them into a tongue shape (Photo 5).

Assembly:

(1) Take 2¾-inch long #20 green wire, tie one flower to the tip with green tape. At 1¼-inch below, symmetrically attach two leaves. Wrap the remaining stem with green tape.

(2) Take 4-inch #20 green wire, tie one flower to the tip with green tape. At 2-inch below, attach a bud and 2 leaves. Wrap the remaining stem with green tape.

(3) Take the thin stem wire, tie one flower to the tip with green tape. At 2-inch below, attach the branches from Step (1) and (2). Wrap the remaining stem with green tape.

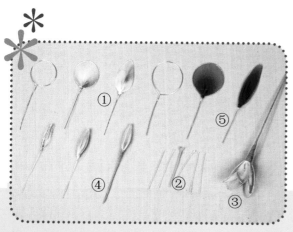

Eustoma

Delphinium (Larkspur)

⌈Materials⌋

#24 silver wire.

Thick stem wire .

White, pink, and purple nylons.

White glue (diluted with water).

Self-made white string stamen (see Page 8 for instructions).

Pink acrylic paint.

Green floral tape.

⌈Instructions⌋

Each Delphinium stalk is tower shaped and has numerous buds and flowers.   Flowers bloom from bottom up along the stalk. Below instructions make 20 flowers and buds.

Petal: Use #24 silver wire to make 107 loops in 1-inch diameter, 110 loops in ¾-inch diameter, each with 1¼-inch handles. Cover loops with nylon in purple nylon. Form loops into oval shape and pinch 2-3 waves along the edge of each loop (Photo 1).

Stamen: Take a piece of purple nylon, wet with glue then allow to dry. Cut ⅛ x 1½-inch strips (Photo 2). Take self-made white string stamen, cut to 1½-inch and dip in pink paint (Photo 3).

Assembly :

(1) Large flower: use thread to tie together (in sequence, from inside-out) five each of type of stamens, five small petals and five large petals.   Wrap handle with green tape (Photo 4).

(2) Medium flower: follow Step (1) using four large petals, three small petals and stamen.

(3) Large bud: follow Step (1) using two small petals and three large petals.

(4) Medium bud: tie together three small petals and wrap handle with green tape. Wrap the three petals tightly together to form the bud.

(5) Entire branch: take thick stem wire, attach a small bud to tip with green tape. Spiral around the stem wire, attach remaining buds and flowers at ¾-inch intervals. The sequence is buds first, from small to large; then flowers, from small to large. Maintain a 1-inch stem on each bud/flower. Wrap remaining stem wire with tape. Create a slight curve in each bud/flower stem.

Delphinium

Gladiolus

「Materials」

#24 silver wire.

Thick stem wire .
Red, pink, white, yellow, pale green or dual-color nylons.

Light green floral tape.
Stamen:
Self-made string stamen.
Self-made string stamen with millet grains attached. (Cover stamen with whiteglue and attach pellets grain or other similar small yellow grain).

「 Instructions 」

Each gladiolus stalk has 3-4 flowers and buds (more can be added if desired).

Petal: (1) Use #24 silver wire to make 12 loops in a 1¾-inch diameter and three loops with 1¾-inch diameter. These loops make four flowers and buds.
Large, blooming flower: six large petals, two layers with 3 petals each.
Half blooming flower: three large petals, one small petal.
Large bud: two large petals, one small petal.
Small bud: one large petal and one small petal.
(2) Select nylon of desired color listed. Cover loops then shape them into oval. Pinch 3-4 waves into petals. For the small bud, roll the petals into cylinder shape after forming the waves. If using dual-color nylon, keep the lighter color to the center and darker color at the edge.
(3) Assemble the blooming flower with three string stamens and one millet covered stamen. The half blooming flower and buds do not require stamen. Keep the flowers half or slightly open (Photo 1).

Leaf: Use #24 silver wire to make five loops with a 1½ inch diameter, four loops with 2-inch diameter, and two loops in 2 ¼-inch diameters. Cover loops with pale green nylon and form them into long, oval shapes (Photo 2).

Assembly: Take the stem wire and cover the top part with light green tape (Photo 3). Attach five leaves, alternating on opposite sides of the stem. Attach a small bud, then cover the bud with a leaf. Attach the big bud on the opposite side of the small bud and cover with large leaf. Use same method to attach all flowers, each covered with a leaf. Finish covering the stem wire with light green floral tape. Crease the leaves slightly and tilt the tips outward.

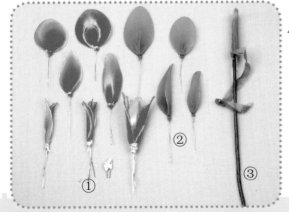

Gladiolus

Agapanthus

「Materials」

#26 silver wire, #22 green wire.

Thick stem wire .

White or lavender nylon.

Light green floral tape.

White, thin nylon thread.

Cotton ball, white glue, orange acrylic paint.

「Instructions」

The instructions below make 50 flowers. Each Agapanthus stalk has 12 blooming flowers, 8 half-open flowers and 30 buds.

Petal: Use #26 silver wire to make 120 loops with a 1-inch diameter. Cover with lavender nylon, keeping the darker nylon near the handle darker. Form loops into oval shapes (Photo 1).

Stamen: Use fingers to rub glue onto the nylon thread. Once dry, cut thread into 1½-inch long segments (you need 72 segments). Dab some orange paint onto one end of each thread segment (Photo 2).

Assemble Flowers:

(1) Take #22 green wire and cut into 50 3-4 inch segments.

(2) Take #26 silver wire and tie six stamens to one end of the wire. Surround the stamens with six petals, arranged in two layers of three petals per layer. The petals should be staggered. Trim off excess wire and wrap with light green tape (Photo 3). Bend the upper half of each petal outward to create a fully blooming flower (Photo 4). Make 12 blooming flowers.

(3) Follow step (2) to make eight half-open flowers. Stamens are not needed. Keep the petals standing upright to create a half-open look.

Assemble Buds: Take a segment of #22 green wire and cotton balls to make 30 buds of varying sizes, following instructions on page 42 for Freesia. When covering cotton balls with nylon, make sure to vary the shade of the buds by adjusting the elasticity of the nylon. Wrap handles with light green tape (Photo 5).

Attach all 50 flowers and buds to the thick stem wire. Blooming flowers should have the longest stem (2 to 2¼-inch long); half-open flowers and buds should have 1 to 1¼-inch long stems. Vary the length of the stems to create an uneven look.

Agapanthus

Agapanthus has an umbrella shape and comes in white or lavender. Each flower has six petals.

51

Kaido Crab Apple

「Materials」

#24 silver wire, #30 green wire
Thin stem wire.
Dark pink – white dual-color,
dark pink, green, dark green
nylons.
Ready-made yellow match stick
stamen.
Brown and green floral tapes
Cotton balls, white glue.

「Instructions」

Buds: Cut #30 green wire into 2¼-inch segments. Use cotton ball and nylon to make buds (see Page 42). These buds are oval shaped and come in three sizes. The small one is the size of a pea and covered in dark pink nylon; the medium bud is soybean sized and covered with dark pink – white dual-color nylon, with an emphasis on the dark-pink. The large bud is peanut sized and covered with three layers of dark pink – white dual-color nylon. Allow the inner layers to peek through, creating the appearance of a bud about to become a flower (Photo 1).

Flower: Blooming flowers have 18 petals, arranged in three layers. Use #24 silver wire to make 12 loops with ¾-inch diameters and six loops with a 1-inch diameter. The small loops are used in the two inner layers and large loops used for the outer layer. Keep a 2 to 2 ½-inch long handle on each loop. Wrap loops in dark pink-white nylon (Photo 2). Stretch loops into oval shapes. Tie the petals and 12 yellow stamens together. Arrange the petals into three layers, with the large petals on the outside. Trim off excess wires, keeping a 2-inch stem and wrap with green tape (Photos 3).

Leaf: Use #24 silver wire to make 1-inch, 1½-inch and 1¾-inch loops. Cover loops with green nylon. There is no need to wrap stems with tape (Photo 4). Form loops into oval shapes and pinch a sharp point on the tip.

Assembly: Take a 11¾-inch long thin stem wire, wrap a couple of passes around one end, then attach 4-5 small, medium and large leaves. Mix in 3-4 small buds with the leaves, maintaining 1½-inch stem on the buds. Continue to wrap brown tape for 1-inch or 1½-inch, then attach a combination of buds, three big/one small, or two small/two medium, or three large/one small. Each cluster of buds and flowers contains 4-6 different sized leaves. Each stalk should include 2-3 clusters. Arrange the leaves so that the flowers or buds are surrounded by leaves. Keep the small buds standing straight up and flowers and big buds bent downward. Bend the entire stem wire slightly as well.

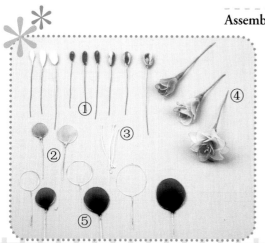

Kaido Crab Apple

Narcissus

「Materials」

#26 silver wire, #22 green wire.
Thin stem wire.
White, egg yellow nylon
Light green floral tape.
White nylon thread.
Ready-made yellow match stick stamen.
White glue.

「Instructions」

Petal: Each flower has six petals and each stalk has 5-7 flowers. Use #26 silver wire to make 1-inch diameter loops in desired quantities. Wrap white nylon around the loops and form them into almond shapes (Photo 5).

Stamen: (1) Cut yellow nylon into 1½-inch wide strips. Brush diluted white glue onto the strip, and wrap the strip around a pen. After the glue dries, cut the rolled up nylon into 1 ½-inch tubes (Photo 1).

(2) Soak a strand of white nylon thread in diluted glue. Let dry and cut into 1½-inch long segments (Photo 2).

(3) Cut #22 green wire into 4 ¾-inch long section. Attach three ready-made yellow string stamens and one white nylon stamen from Step (2) to one end of the green wire (Photo 3). Loop a yellow tube (from Step (1)) over the stamens and cinch the bottom of the tube (Photo 4).

Assembly:

(1) Wrap six petals around the assembled stamen. Arrange the petals into two layers. Trim off excess wire. Use pliers to flatten down the wires then wrap stem with light green tape (Photo 6).

(2) Take thin stem wire and attach one flower to one end. Then attach 4-6 more flowers at the same spot, leaving a 1¼-inch long stem on each flower. Trim off excess wire and wrap the rest of the stem wire with light green tape.

Final Touches:

(1) use the tip of a pen to open up the yellow tube into cone shape.

(2) Narcissus is umbrella shaped. Bend the flowers downward slightly and spread them out.

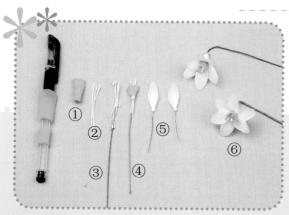

Narcissus

Chinese Lantern

⌈Materials⌋

#26 silver wire.
#22 green wire.
Thin stem wire .
Green and orange-yellow dual-color nylons.
Green floral tape.
White nylon thread.
White florist foam block.

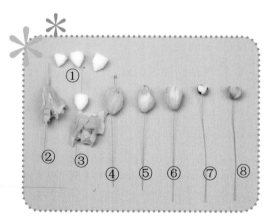

⌈Instructions⌋

Flower: (1) Use a knife to cut and shape foam block into small cones. Each cone has a ¾-inch diameter base and is about 1-inch tall. Try to vary the size of the cones slightly. Dig a small hole at the base of the cone (Photo 1).

(2) Cut #22 green wire into 3 1/4 to 4-inch long sections and cut orange-yellow nylon into 4-inch squares.

(3) Pierce a green wire section through the middle of the square nylon. Cinch the nylon around the wire. Becareful to not cinch too tightly (Photo 2).

(4) Use the tip of the wire from Step (3) to piece a foam cone with the base of the cone up. Bend the wire at the tip to form a small loop (Photo 3).

(5) Flip the nylon square around to cover the foam cone loosely and tie up the open end. Do not wrap the nylon too tightly around the cone (Photo 4).

(6) Push the enclosed foam cone toward the small loop at the tip of the wire. Stop when the small loop is nestled in the small hole at the base of the cone (Photo 5). Arrange the wrinkles in the nylon evenly to make it look like a lantern. This completes a lantern flower.

(7) Make buds using the same method as above. Chinese Lantern buds are really just flowers that have not yet matured and changed color. Use slightly smaller foam cones and use green nylon (Photos 7, 8).

Leaf: Use green #22 wire to make nine 1 ½ -inch to 2-inch diameter loops. Cover loops with green nylon. Form loops into oval shape and pinch the top of the loop into a sharp point. Bend the leaf to create a valley in the middle.

Assembly: Attach two small leaves to the tip of the thin stem wire. Continue to attach leaves, buds and flowers in clusters of one leaf, one flower/bud or two leafs and two flowers/buds. The space between clusters increases gradually from top to bottom (from ¾ to 2-inch); the size of leaves and flowers also increases going down. The length of the stems for the flower and leaves also increases, from ¾-inch at the top to 2⅓-inch at the bottom.

Chinese Lantern

Each stalk of Chinese Lantern has about seven flowers and buds.

Bird of Paradise

「Materials」

#26 silver wire, #20 or 22 green wire.

Thick stem wire .

Orange, purple and green nylons.

Green, yellow, and red floral tapes.

White nylon thread.

Purple nylon thread (or you can use strips of purple nylon).

「Instructions」

Flower: (1) Use #26 silver wire to make six 2 ¼-inch loops, maintaining a 1½-inch long handle on each loop. Use #20 or #22 green wire to make one 4-inch diameter loop for the leaf and one 3 ½-inch loop for the receptacle (Photo 1).

(2) Cover four silver loops with orange nylon, form them into oval shapes and fold the oval lengthwise in half (Photo 2). Cover the other two silver loops in purple nylon, form them into an oval shape and fold the oval lengthwise in half, then pinch them into arrow shapes (Photo 3). Tie the bottom portion of the arrow with purple nylon.

(3) Cover the two types of green loops with green nylon, form them into oval shapes and fold the oval in half lengthwise. The long one is the receptacle (Photo 4), the short one is the leaf.

Assembly: (1) Tie the two orange petals and one purple petal together to the thick stem wire using thick nylon thread, with the purple petal in the center. Wrap the handle with red tape to complete the flower (Photo 5).

(2) Repeat Step (1) to make another flower. After wrapping ¾-inch of the handle with red tape, add the other flower and wrap another 1¼-inch of red tape. Then switch to yellow tape and continue to wrap the stem for about 1¾-inch. Attach the receptacle and switch to green tape to wrap 1½-inch. Attach two green leaves, then finish wrapping the stem with green tape.

Each Bird of Paradise stalk has two to three flowers. Each flower has two orange petals and one purple petal. Its receptacle is multi-colored and unique;

Bird of Paradise

When assembling the receptacle, make sure the front petal of the first flower lies sideways so that the tip of the petal is parallel to the receptacle. The receptacle should shield the red floral tape covering the stem. When attaching the leaf, the top portion of the leaf should cover the base of the receptacle.

Chrysanthemum

⌈Materials⌋

#24 silver wire, #20 green wire

Thin stem wire

White, pale yellow, yellow, orange, light green, grassy green and green nylons.

Ready-made button style stamen in yellow and green.

Green floral tapes.

White glue (diluted with half water)

⌈Instructions⌋

Petal:

(1) Select 8-inch long nylon in desired color and cut a straight line to slice open the nylon tube. Fold the rectangular nylon lengthwise in half, twice. (Photo 1). Hold down and flatten the folded nylon and cut a 3/8-inch strip lengthwise.

(2) Soak the strip in diluted glue (½ glue and ½ water). Use thumb and forefinger to squeeze out the excess liquid. Hold both ends of the strip and stretch to 1.5 to 2 times its original length. Put the stretched nylon strip on a flat surface (such as a cutting board to dry).

Stamen: Use the same method as for the petal to make strip for stamen. Select a nylon that is a darker shade of the petal color. When the strip is half dry, wrap the strip around a pen or pencil, then let dry to create a spiral (Photo 2).

Leaf: Use #24 silver wire to make 1¼ - to 1½-inch diameter loops (six to nine leaves per stalk). Cover the loops with green nylon then form them into leaf shape. Take a 2 ½ - to 3 ⅛-inch long #20 green wire and attach one leaf to one end with green tape. Attach two more leaves ½-inch down the wire. Wrap the rest of the wire with green tape. This forms a small leaf branch.

Assembly: (1) Cut the petal strip into 2 ¾ to 3–inch sections. Cut the stamen strip into 1½ to 2-inch sections.

(2) Take #20 green wire and fold it in half. Thread the green wire through the button stamen (Photo 3). Attach 20-25 stamen strips around the button. Surround the stamen with 30-40 petal strips. Trim the tips to keep them slightly uneven.

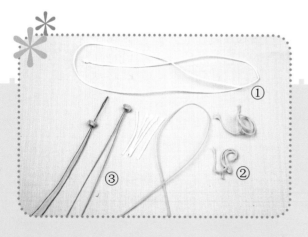

Chrysanthemum

Calla Lily

⌈Materials⌋

#18 green and white wires.

Thin and thick stem wires.

White, yellow, red, pink, orange, green, and green-white dual-color nylons.

Ready-made button style stamen in yellow and green.

Light green and yellow floral tapes.

White nylon thread.

⌈Instructions⌋

Flower: (1) Take #18 white or green wire and make 5 ½ -inch diameter loop, maintaining a 3 to 4-inch long handle (Photo 1).

(2) Wrap the nylon around the loop. Use your left thumb and middle finger to hold one end of the nylon to the base of the loop; use the left forefinger to aid the right hand to pull the nylon up, forcing the loop to become more circular. Tie off the nylon (Photo 2).

(3) Form the loop into a peach shape. Pinch waves into the pointy end of the peach shape.

(4) Using a pen or pencil as a guide, roll the bottom of the petal around the pencil to form a funnel (Photo 3).

Assembly: Take the thick stem wire and wrap yellow tape around one end several times (colored calla lilies are smaller than white calla lily. The stamen is less visible so a hint of yellow tip is sufficient). Thread the yellow tape-covered wire stem through the funnel shaped flower. Wrap light green tape around the stem wire, starting thicker at the top and gradually thinning out below.

Calla Lily

Crape-Myrtle

⌈Materials⌋

#24 silver wire.
#30 green wire.
#20 green wire.
Thin stem wire.
Green, brown, white, pink, dark pink, lavender nylons (you can use scrap nylon pieces).
Green and brown floral tapes.
White light-weight beads/balls, with an approximate 1/8-inch diameter.

⌈Instructions⌋

Bud: Take white beads and cover with green or brown nylon. Keep nylon handle for two of the beads and trim off excess nylon from the rest (Photo 1).

Flower: Cut #30 green wire into 4- to 4 ¾-inch sections. Cut all nylons into ¼ by 1⅜-inch long strips. Use the Baby's Breath method (Page 34) to make single flowers. Trim the strips on the flower into different lengths (Photo 2). The flowers on each stalk need to have the same color.

Leaf : Take #24 silver wire and make ¾ to 1-inch diameter loops. Cover with green wire and form into leaf shapes (Photo 3).

Assembly: Cut #20 green wire into 6- to 8-inch long section. Attach one brown bud to the tip of the wire using brown tape. Attach another 3-7 buds below the first bud. Use green tape if the buds are green instead of brown. Then attach 5-7 flowers, gradually increasing the length of the flower stem (Photo 4).

Attach 2-3 stalks of flowers and leaves to the thin stem wire.

Crape-Myrtle

Acacia

⌈Materials⌋

#18 silver wire.
#30 green wire.
Thin stem wire.
Golden yellow nylon.
Green floral tapes.

⌈Instructions⌋

Petal: Take golden yellow nylon and cut into 1/8 x 1 ¼-inch strips. Take #30 green wire and cut 1 ¼-inch, 1 ½-inch, 2-inch, 2 ¼-inch, and 2 ¾-inch length sections. Use instructions for Baby's Breath (Page 34) to make desired quantity of flowers. More strips will be used than for Baby's Breath. Trim the flowers into ⅜-inch balls.

Assembly: (1) Cut #20 green wire into 4- , 6-, and 8-inch long sections. Attach flowers to a green wire section using green tape. Flowers should be about ⅜-inch apart. Leave the bottom 2-inch of the green wire without any flowers and wrap only with tape. The stems on each individual flower should vary in length from ⅜-inch (at the top) to 2 ¾-inch (at the bottom).

(2)Taking a thin stem wire, attach the shortest stalks first, then continue to attach stalks spaced 1 ¼-inch to 1 ½-inch apart. Finish wrapping the stem wire with tape. The overall shape of the Acacia is a triangle.

Sleepy Morning

⌈Materials⌋

#18, #28 green wire and #24 silver wire.
Pale green, grassy green and golden yellow nylons.
Light green floral tapes.

⌈Instructions⌋

Flower:

Take #28 green wire, cut into 2-inch and 2 ¾-inch sections until you have a total of 20. Cut pale green and golden yellow nylon into ¼ inch x 1 ¼-inch long strips. Take the 2 ¾-inch green wire sections and the pale green nylon and follow instructions for Baby's Breath on Page 34 to make same sized flowers in desired quantity. These green flowers are buds. Take the 2-inch green wire sections and golden yellow nylon and make flowers of various sizes in desired quantity. Wrap the stem with light green tape.

Leaf:

Take #24 silver wire to make 1 ¼-inch and 1 ½ -inch diameter loops, for a total of three each. Wrap loops in grassy green nylon and form them into leaf shapes. Pinch a few waves into the leaf edges and curve the leaves slightly.

Assembly:

Take 11¾-inch long #18 green wire and tie three green buds to the tip using light green tape; Keep about a 1-inch stem on the buds. Continue to attach flowers and leaves. Lastly, attach three large leaves, about ⅜-inch apart. Use light green tape to finish wrapping the green wire.

67

Lace Flower

「Materials」

#28 green wire.
Thin stem wire.
White nylon (can use scrap nylon).
Green floral tapes.

「Instructions」

Lace flowers are white and are arranged in an umbrella shape. The flowers are small and stems are thin. Each stalk has 40-50 flowers.

Flower:

Take #28 green wire, cut 50 sections of various lengths, from 2¼-inch to 5¼-inch. Cut white nylon into 1/8-inch x 1⅜-inch long strips. Follow instructions for Baby's Breath on Page 34 to make lace flowers, but use more white nylon strips. Trim flowers to just under ½-inch.

Assembly:

Attach 40-50 flowers to one end of a thin stem wire. Arrange the flowers into an umbrella shape and trim off unnecessary wires. Use green tape to wrap the rest of the stem wire.

Final Touches:

Keep each flower standing straight in all directions.

Forget-Me-Not

⌈Materials⌋

#20 and #30 green wire
Purple and lavender nylons.
Green floral tapes.

⌈Instructions⌋

Flower: Cut #30 green wire into various lengths, from 3¼ - to 4¾-inch long. Cut nylons in both colors into roughly ⅛-inch x 1 ½-inch strips (Photo 1). Follow instructions from Baby's Breath on Page 34. Forget-Me-Not flowers are bigger than Baby's Breath and use slightly more strips (Photo 2). Each stalk has 12- 14 flowers. The stems of the first 3-4 flowers do not need to be covered with green tape. The remaining flowers should have their stems wrapped in green tape of various lengths, ¾, 1, 1¼, 2 and 2 ¼-inch.

Assembly: (1) Take a piece of #20 green wire and attach a flower at one end. Then attach 3-4 more flowers. These flowers do not have stems. Subsequent flowers should have gradually longer stems. The flowers should be arranged in matching pairs, forming two rows on the green wire. The spacing between pairs of flowers should be gradually increased from ½-inch to 1 ¼-inch apart.

(2) Take two assembled stalks, wrap the bottom portion of the stalks together with green tape. Bend one stalk just below the last flower so the two stalks form a "L" shape.

Cosmos

「Materials」

#24 silver wire. Thin stem wire (11¾-inch long).
Yellow, orange, pale blue, pink, purple nylons.
Green floral tapes.
Ready-made button style stamen in yellow, orange and green.

「Instructions」

Petal: Use #24 silver wire to make eight 1¼-inch or 1½-inch diameter loops. Wrap the loops in desired nylon color (Photo 1). Stretch the loops to elongate them, with the top end wider than the bottom (the end with handle). Pinch three teeth at the tip of each petal (Photo 2).

Stamen: Bend a 4-inch long silver wire, bend into "U" shape. Thread a button stamen through the wire until it reaches the bottom of the "U". Squeeze the two sections of the wire together to close off the "U" (Photo 3).

Assembly: Tie the stamen assembly to one end of the thin stem wire. Arrange and stagger eight petals around the button stamen.

Chinese Asparagus

「Materials」

#22 and #30 green wire. Green floral tape.

「Instructions」

1.Cut #30 green wire into ½ inch to ¾ inch long sticks to make Chinese Asparagus needles (Photo 1)

2. Take another piece of #30 green wire, fold it in half. Twist the needles onto the green wire such that the middle of the needles intersect the wire (Photo 2). Use scissors to trim the needles, with the needles gradually getting longer going from one end to the other. Turn the needles in different directions (Photo 3).

3. Take 10 strands of needles of various lengths, attach them to the #22 green wire. Arrange the strands such that the longest strands on top and the shortest strands are on the botton.

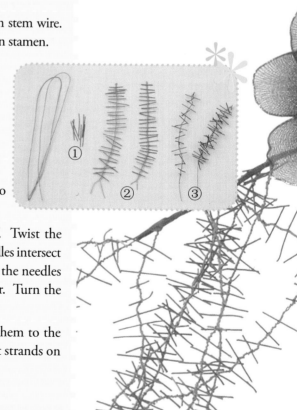

Cosmos comes in various colors and the sizes. Each flower has eight petals.

Gomphrena Strawberry Fields

「Materials」

#26 silver wire, #20 green wire (11 to 12-inch long).
Red or burgundy, green nylon.
Green floral tape.

「Instructions」

Flower: Cut red or burgundy nylon into ⅛-inch x 1 ¼-inch strips. Follow instructions from Baby's Breath on Page 34 to make the flowers. Trim flowers to ½-inch diameter. Use only one color of nylon per flower.

Leaf : Use #26 silver wire to make ¾-inch diameter loops (each flower has two leaves). Wrap the loops in green nylon and form them into leaf shape. Attach two leaves to a flower using green tape. The leaves should be opposite each other. There is no need to wrap the wire with tape.

Assembly: Tie the stamen assembly to one end of the thin stem wire. Arrange and stagger eight petals around the button stamen. Trim off excess wires and use green tape to cover the entire stem wire. Gomphrena flowers are long-lasting and the leaves often fall off first. So the leaves can be omitted.

Gold Dust Dracaena

「Materials」

#24 silver wire, #20 green wire (12 to 15-inch).
Green nylon.
Green floral tape; orange acrylic paint.

「Instructions」

Leaf: Use #24 silver wire to make 1¼ -inch to 2-inch diameter loops (Photo 1). Wrap the loops in green nylon and form them into leaf shape (Photo 2). Paint a few orange small spots on each leaf (Photo 3).

Assembly: After the paint dries, attach leaves to #20 green wire. Attach one leaf at one end. Assemble 2-3 leaves together with green tape, then attach the assembly to the green wire stem. Leaves or clusters of leaves should be spaced 2 to 2 ¼-inch apart on the wire.

Amarantus Tricolor

⌜Materials⌟

#24 silver wire, #28 green wire, thin stem wire.
Red, deep red nylon.
Red and brown floral tapes. Black ink.

⌜Instructions⌟

Flower Stalk: (1) Cut red nylon into ⅛-inch x 1 ¼-inch strips. Take #28 wire, fold in half. Insert a few strips of nylon between the wires into the fold. Twist the wires a couple of times to secure the strips. Insert more strips, then twist wires again. Continue until only 1 ½-inch of wire is left at the bottom. Make more stalks in 4-inch, 6-inch, and 8-inch lengths, two of each. Pull/stretch the nylon strips with your fingers, then trim the nylon so the stalk is about ¾-inch in diameter, with the narrowest portion of the stick at the top with a pointed tip.

(2) Take the thin stem wire, wrap about ½-inch of one-end in red tape. Then attach the longest stalk to the stem wire. Continue to wrap stem wire with red tape for about 1-inch, then attach the 8-inch stalks on each side of the stem wire. Attach the remaining pairs of stalks, from long to short, spaced about ½-inch apart. Wrap the rest of the stem wire with red tape.

Leaf: Use #24 silver wire to make four loops each in 1 ¼-inch, 1 ½-inch, 2-inch, and 2 ¼-inch diameters (Photo 1). Maintain a 1 ½-inch handle for each loop. Wrap 1 ¼-inch and 1 ½-inch loops in red nylon, 2-inch and 2 ¼-inch loops in burgundy nylon (Photo 2). Form loops into leaf shape, and pinch a few waves around the tip of the leaves (Photo 3). Stretch the leaves length-wise to cause the leaves to curve slightly inward. Wrap the handle of each leave with red tape.

Assembly: (1) Take a thin stem wire, attach a small red leaf to the tip with red tape, maintain 3/8-inch stem on the leaf. Twist the red leaf slightly. Attach two more small red leaves on each side of the stem wire. 3/8-inch away, attach the fourth leaf. Attach the remaining red leaves in the same manner, from small leaves to large, gradually keeping longer leaf stems, from 3/8-inch to ¾-inch. Wrap the rest of the thin stem wire with brown tape.

(2) Use a small paint brush to tint the tip of each leaf slightly. Amarantus Tricolor flower stalks grow from the tip of the of the leaf branch. But the flower stalks are too heavy and too long to be attached to the leave branch. Arrange the flowers and leaves separately in the vase.

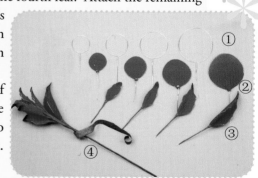

Sanguisorba

「Materials」
#20 green wire.
Rust red, olive or green nylon.

「Instructions」
Cut each color nylon into 1/8-inch x 1 ¼-inch strips. Take #20 green wire, bend a hook at one end. Insert a good amount of strips into the hook then twist the hook closed to secure the nylon strips. Trim off excess wire. Pull and stretch the nylon strips, then trim the nylon strips. Do not mix nylon colors.

Winterberry

⌈Materials⌋

White light-weight beads/balls, about ⅛-inch diameter.

White glue.

Red nylon; red nylon thread.

#30 brown wire.

Rattan vine.

⌈Instructions⌋

1. Trim and clean the vine, wash and dry. Punch 2-3 small holes where the vine splits off.

2. Wrap the white beads in double-layer of red nylon and cinch close with nylon thread. Trip off excess nylon (Photo 1).

3. Cut #30 brown wire into 1 ¼-inch long sections. Dip the tip in white glue, then pierce the glue end into red nylon covered ball. Dip the other end in glue and insert it into one of the holes in the rattan vine (Photo 2).

Poinsettias

「Materials」

#24 silver wire.

Thin stem wire (8-inch long).

Green, red, yellow nylon.

Red floral tape, white glue.

「Instructions」

Petal: Use #24 silver wire to make 1 ½-inch to 1 ¾-inch loops, keeping 1 ¼-inch to 2-inch long handle on each loop. Wrap loops in red nylon, and form them into leaf shape. Cover handles with red tape (Photo 1).

Bud: Wrap red and yellow scrap or strips with green nylon to form various size balls. Make 10 balls. Apply a small amount of glue on a few balls. After the glue dries, cut a small opening in the ball to expose some of the red and yellow nylon inside. Tie the balls into a cluster.

Assembly: Attach the buds to a thin stem wire with red tape. Surround the buds with about 10 petals. Arrange the leaves in two layers, with the smaller leaves on the inside. Leave a bit of red stem showing on each petal.

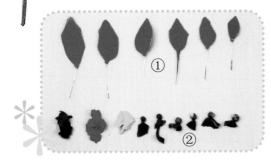

Poinsettias petals are actually leaves that turn from green to red. The petals/leaves come in different sizes and shapes. Some of them have sharp edges and corners. Each flower has 15-18 petals. When assembling the flowers, try to keep the form irregular and do not try to achieve a perfect circle.

Pine

「Materials」

#20 and #30 green wire.

Thin stem wire.

Brown floral tape.

「Instructions」

Branch: (1) Cut #30 green wire into 20-30 sections, 2-inch to 2 ¾-inch long (Photo 1).

(2) Cut #20 green wire into 6-inch long sections (Photo 1).

(3) Take a 6-inch #20 green wire section (branch), attach 10-15 #20 green wire sections (needles) to the top using brown tape (Photo 3). Continue to attach needle clusters along the branch. Wrap the tape several times when attaching the needles. Using both sides of the branch. Leave about 2-inch to 2 ¾-inch of the branch at the bottom bare of needles (Photo 4).

Assembly: Take thin stem wire, attach a few needles to one end with brown tape (Photo 5). Then attach small branches to the stem wire. Keep the spacing between these branches uneven. Keep 4 to 6-inch of stem wire at the bottom bare of branches (Photo 6).

Vary the length and shape of each branch to create a more natural look.

Clematis

⌈Materials⌋

#24 silver wire, #20 green wire.

Thin stem wire (8-inch long).

Light purple, pink, burgundy nylon.

dark pink or dual-color nylon in similar shades.

White glue (diluted with water 50/50).

White and yellow nylon thread.

⌈Instructions⌋

Petal: Use #24 silver wire to make 1 ½-inch loops, six to eight per flower. Wrap loops in nylon. Clematis petals have faint patterns toward the center of the flowers. Try to form a few long wrinkles to mimic the pattern. Form loops into long oval shape and pinch a sharp point at the tip (Photo 1).

Stamen: Clematis has 30-40 stamens. They are white or yellow and look like string (they can be slightly wavy). Soak white and yellow nylon threads (or thick cotton thread) in diluted glue. Hang dry then cut into about 1-inch length (Photo 2).

Assembly: Take #20 green wire, tie roughly 10 stamens to the tip, leave about ½-inch above the tip (Photo 3). Apply a small amount of glue to the bottom portion of the stamen bunch, then add another 20-30 stamens around it. Surround the stamen with 6-8 petals. Trim off excess wire and wrap the rest of the green wire stem with green tape (Photo 3).

Silver Vine

⌜Materials⌟

#24 silver wire.

#20 green wire.

Grassy green nylon.

Light green floral tape.

⌜Instructions⌟

Leaf: Using #24 silver wire, make 11 loops in 2-inch diameter. Keep 1¼-inch to 1½-inch handle on the loops. Wrap loops with nylon then form the loops into triangular shape. Wrap handles with light green tape (Photo 1).

Assembly: Attach a leaf to the tip of #20 green wire using light green tape. Twist the leaf length-wise slightly. Continue to attach leaves around the wire, maintaining a ¾-inch space between leaves. Attach all 11 leaves to the wire (Photo 2).

Blazing-star

⌈Materials⌋

#30 green wire.
Thick stem wire.
Green, dark pink nylon.
Green floral tape.
White glue (diluted with water 50/50).

⌈Instructions⌋

Flower: Cut #30 green wire into 4-inch sections. Cut green nylon and dark pink into ¼-inch x 1 ¼-inch strips (Photos 1,2). Use the wire sections and nylon strips, following instructions for Baby's Breath (Page 34) to make small flowers. Make flowers with three different color combinations – all dark pink (Photo 3), 2/3 dark pink and 1/3 green (Photo 4), 1/3 dark pink and 2/3 green (Photo 5).

Leaf: Take a sheet of green nylon (can also use scrap pieces) and wet with diluted glue. Dry flat then cut into 1/8-inch x 1 ¼-inch strips (Photo 6).

Assembly: Attach flowers in Photos 3, 4, and 5 around the thick stem wire in sequence. When attaching flowers from Photo 5, start mixing in leaves. Finally attach leaves only for about 2-4 inches.

Spotted Dumbcane

⌈Materials⌋

#20 or #22 green wire.
Light yellow nylon.
Green floral tape.
Green acrylic paint.

⌈Instructions⌋

1. Use green wire to make 2 ¼-inch to 4-inch diameter loops in desired quantity, maintain about 2-inch handle on loops.

2. Wrap loops in light yellow nylon then form them into leaf shape (Photo 1). Wrap handles with green tape (Photo 2).

3. Paint the leaves around the edges with green paint (Photo 2).

Chrysanthemum Indicum

「Materials」

#24 silver wire.

#20 and #22 green wire.

Thin stem wire.

Green, light green, pale yellow, yellow, orange, light green-white dual color nylons.

Green floral tape.

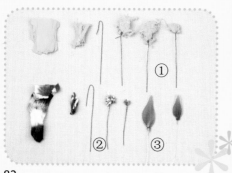

「Instructions」

Flower: Take #22 green wire, pale yellow, yellow and orange nylon to make flowers following directions from Forget-Me-Not (Page 69). Maintain 2 to 4-inch long stem. Do not wrap in tape (Photo 1).

Bud: Cut light green or dual-color nylon into strips. Use same method to make slightly smaller flowers (Photo 2).

Leaf: Use #24 silver wire to make ¾-inch to 1¼-inch diameter loops. Wrap loops with green nylon then form loops into leaf shape (Photo 3).

Assembly: Take #20 green wire and attach flowers, buds and leaves to the wire to make flower stalk, 4 to 8-inch long. Use 7:3:2 ratio of flowers, buds and leaves for each stalk. Attach 3-5 stalks to the thin stem wire.

Plumeria

「Materials」

#24 silver wire.
Thin stem wire.
White and light green nylon.
Brown and green floral tape.
Yellow acrylic paint.
White glue.

「Instructions」

Petal: Each flower has six petals. Use #24 silver wire to make six 1 ½-inch diameter loops. Wrap loops in white nylon and form them into olive shapes. Paint the portion of the leaves that will be at the center of the Plumeria with yellow paint (Photo 1).

Bud: Follow instructions for Polianthes Tuberrosa on Page 38 to make buds. But instead cover buds with light green nylon (Photo 2).

Assembly: Wrap light green tape around the tip of the thin stem wire several times. Stagger six petals around the tip of the stem wire. Wrap stem with brown tape. Assemble 2-3 buds together then combine with flower stem to make a stalk.

Donkey Tail

⌈Materials⌋

#20 green wire.
Light green tape.
Light green nylon.
Cotton pads.
White glue .
White cotton thread.

⌈Instructions⌋

Succulent Leaf:

(1) Cut cotton pads into pieces about size of two thumbs. Apply a small amount of glue, then roll up the pieces with a knitting needle into a long cylinder with sharp tip (Photo 1).

(2) With the knitting needle still inside, wrap the little cylinders with light green nylon. Pinch the tip of the needle to the top of the cylinder to prevent the needle from poking through the nylon. Make sure the nylon is taut around the cotton cylinder. Cinch the nylon with cotton thread (not too tightly) and keep about 1-inch of extra nylon "tail" (Photon 2).

(3) Pinching the tip of the cylinder with one hand, pull out the knitting needle with the other hand. Use nylon thread to tightly cinch close the nylon (Photo 3). It is necessary to keep the knitting needle in to give the cotton cylinder some stiffness so the nylon can be pulled tautly. The green nylon should appear almost white at the tip.

(4) Roll the cylinder between palms a few times to form the cylinder into a long olive shape. The glue inside the cotton will help maintain the shape (Photo 4).

(5) Trim off the excess nylon from the leaf, keeping a small strip for tying purposes (Photo 5). Make 30-50 leaves or more if desired.

Wait for the glue inside the cotton to dry before proceeding with assembly.

Assembly: Take #20 green wire, attach leaves around the wire using light green tape, starting at the tip. Increase the size of the leaves gradually. Apply glue to the excess nylon on the leaves to help keep them down.

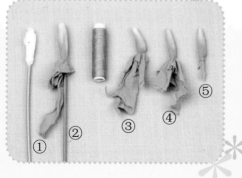

Donkey Tail

Rosary Vine

⌈Materials⌋

#28 or #30 green or brown wire.
Light green tape.
Green, maroon, burgundy, burnt umber or dual-color in similar shades nylons.
Brown floral tape.
White glue (diluted with water 50/50).

⌈Instructions⌋

Leaf: Cut #30 wire into 1¼-inch to 1½-inch long sections (Photo 1). Wet green or maroon nylon with diluted glue. Lay wire sections on top of the wet nylon, about 1 ¼-inch apart. Leave ½ length of the wire section on top of the nylon and ½ off (Photon 2). Put a different colored wet nylon on top of the wires. After the nylon layers are dry, cut out heart shaped leaves with the wires at the center of each leaf. Vary the size of the leaves (Photo 3).

Assembly: Take #28 or #30 green wire and tie a small leaf to the tip with brown tape. Continue to attach leaves at ¼ to ½-inch intervals apart (alternating sides) until there is 4 to 6-inch of stem left. Wrap the rest of the stem with brown tape.

Take 6 to 8-inch long #28 or #30 wire, attach a few already assembled short branches, then attach individual leaves to the long wire.

Rosary Vine

Eucalyptus

「Materials」

#24 silver wire, #20 green wire.
Lime green, green, or grayish green nylon.
Green floral tape.

「Instructions」

Leaf: Use #24 silver wire to make ¾-inch and 1¼-inch loops. Cover the small loops with lime green nylon and large loops with green nylon (Photo 1).

Assembly: Take #20 green wire, attach one small leaf to the tip with green floral tape, continue to attach leaves in pairs at about ¾ to 1¼-inch apart. Adjacent pairs should be offset and have different orientations.

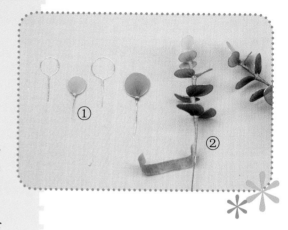

Red Eucalyptus

「Materials」

#24 silver wire, #18 green wire.
Maroon, mustard yellow or dual-color in similar shades nylons.
Red and brown floral tapes.

「Instructions」

Leaf: Use #24 silver wire to make 1 ½-inch, 2-inch and 2 ¼-inch loops (Photo 1). Cover the loops with nylon and form them into triangular leaf shape (Photos 2, 3). Cover the stem of each leaf with about ½-inch of red tape (Photo 4).

Assembly: Take #18 green wire, attach one small leaf to the tip with brown floral tape. Continue to attach leaves on the same side of the wire at ¾-inch to 1 ¼-inch apart. Sequence the leaves from small to large. Leave about 10-inch long stem and wrap it with brown tape.

Red Eucalyptus

Eucalyptus

89

Polka Dot Plant

「Materials」

#24 silver wire.
#20 green wire
(8 to 10-inch long).
Burgundy nylon.
Green floral tape.
Green acrylic paint.

「Instructions」

(1) Use #24 silver wire to make 1-inch, 1 ¼ -inch and 1 ½ -inch loops. Cover loops with burgundy nylon then form them into leaf shape (Photo 1,2).

(2) Take #20 green wire, tape a small leaf at the tip, then attach leaves around the wire at ¾-inch to ¼-inch apart. Sequence the leaves from small to large. Attach 8 to 9 leaves then wrap the rest of the wire with green floral tape (Photo 3).

(3) Use small brush and green acrylic paint to paint out the vein patterns on the leaves.

Eurasian Smoketree

「Materials」

#24 silver wire.
#20 green wire.
Reddish brown, chartreuse,
maroon nylons.
Green floral tapes.

「Instructions」

Leaf: Use #24 silver wire to make 16 loops in 2-inch to 2 ¼-inch diameter, keep 1 ½-inch to 2-inch handles on the loops. Wrap the loops with nylon in listed colors. Form loops into peach shape and cover about ¾-inch of the handles with green tape. Use green tape to wrap pairs of leaves together.

Assembly: Take #20 green wire, attach a pair of pre-assembled leaves to the tip. Attach another pair 1 ¼-inch away. Then continue to attach the rest of the leaf pairs at 1 ½ to 2-inch intervals apart until all leaves are attached.

Final Touches: When combining leaves into pairs, mix up the colors as desired. Curve the stem of each leave up slightly and point the tips of the leaves in different direction.

91

Cattail

⌈Materials⌋

Thick, thin stem wires.
Brown nylon (cut into 5 ½-inch x 4 ¾-inch rectangle pieces).
Newspaper (cut into 4 ¾-inch wide strips).
Cotton batting (cut into 4 ¾-inch x 4-inch rectangles. Pull to thin sheet).
White glue (diluted with water 50/50).

⌈Instructions⌋

1. Wrap about 1-inch of the tip of a thick stem wire with light green tape. Keep some slack in the tape so the tape can be pinched into a sharp point at the tip. Continue to wrap the rest of the stem wire.

2. At about ½-inch from the tip, apply glue to the stem wire (if using thin stem wire, leave 1 ½-inch at the tip). Wrap the newspaper strips around the stem wire and apply glue as needed. Do not wrap the newspaper too tightly. Form a cylinder with about 1-inch diameter.

3. Lay a nylon piece on a flat surface, center a cotton sheet on top of the nylon. The nylon should be about ⅜-inch larger than the cotton sheet on all four sides. Brush the nylon and cotton sheet edges with glue. Put the newspaper cylinder on top of the cotton/nylon. Wrap the cotton/nylon evenly around the cylinder.

4. Bring the assembled stalk upright, apply additional glue to the nylon to secure the edges. Tuck any excess nylon under the top and bottom of the newspaper cylinder. Let glue dry.

Pussy Willow

⌈Materials⌋

#24, #26 or #28 wire (any color, you can use scrap).
Thick or thin stem wire.
White and brown nylon.
Brown floral tape.
Cotton ball.
White glue.

⌈Instructions⌋

1. Cut thin wire into 1 ¼-inch sections. Attach cotton to the wire section with glue to form desired quantity of bean sized and peanuts sized buds. Wrap white or brown nylon around the buds. Trim off excess nylon (Photos 1, 2).

2. Attach buds around thick or thin stem wire using brown tape. Keep ¾-inch to 1 ¼-inch space between buds. The bottom 8 inches of the stem wire should be bare of buds and covered with brown tape only. Each branch should contain single color buds.

Do not mix different color buds.

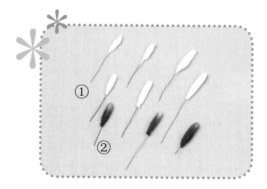

Ivy

⌈Materials⌋

#22 green wire.

#30 green wire (cut into 3 to 3 ½ -inch sections).

Green-yellow or green-white dual-color nylon.

Light green and brown floral tapes.

White glue (diluted with water 50/50).

⌈Instructions⌋

Ivy leaves are small and each leaf has three points.

1. Cut nylon into four pieces. Wet with diluted glue then lay the pieces on a flat surface (Photo 1). Put the #30 green wire sections on the wet nylon, keeping about 1-inch on top of the nylon and the rest of the wire off the nylon. (Photo 2).

2. Alternate sides when laying down the wire sections. Space the wire sections 1 ½-inch to 2 ¼-inch apart (Photo 3). Put another piece of wet nylon on top of the wires. Flatten the nylon pieces to ensure there are no bubbles in between. Once the nylon dries, cut out ivy shaped leaves. There is no need to wrap the leaf stems with floral tape.

3. Attach the leaves to #22 green wire using light green and brown tapes. Sequence the leaves from small to big.

① ② ③

String of Pearls

「Materials」

Deep green nylon.
Small polystyrene foam (Styrofoam) balls
(about 3/8 to ¼-inch diameter).
Green nylon thread.
Green floral tapes.

「Instructions」

1. Wrap the foam balls with double
layers of green nylon and tie off with
green nylon thread. Be sure to tie the
thread tightly. Trim off excess nylon
(Photo 1).

2. Fold the nylon thread in half and
thread the folded end through a needle.
Pull the folded end even with the other
ends so the four strands are of the same
length. Apply small amount of glue
to the thread using your thumb and
forefinger. String the green balls together
using the needle and four-strands of
thread. Thread through the little knot on
the balls, rather than through the balls .
If different size balls are used, thread the
balls from small to large.

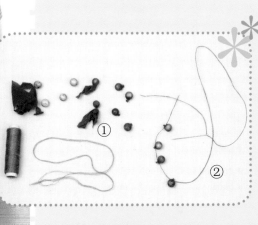